New houses 1

Decorators' Tour

Tina Skinner

Design!

If you're interested in architecture, landscaping, graphic design, fashion or any other form of the visual arts, we've got hundreds of inspiring books. Schiffer Publishing, Ltd. has worked hard to cultivate a broad backlist of titles, each packed to the endpages with visual stimulation. You simply get more pictures per page, more pages per book, and better color reproduction and book production quality than most publishing houses are willing to invest in. Our sumptuous books are worth every penny, because we've spent millions making sure that you find inspiring color and detail every time you open the covers.

Be sure to get our print catalogs with over 3,200 titles by calling U.S. 610-593-1777, or visit our website at:
www.schifferbooks.com.
Most importantly, be sure to support your local book dealers when it is time to expand your library.

L-3

Schiffer Publishing Ltd

4880 Lower Valley Road, Atglen, Pa 19310

Other Schiffer Books by Tina Skinner

Showhouse Review: An Exposé of Interior Decorating Events. ISBN: 9780764328640. $44.95

Other Schiffer Books on Related Subjects

California Revival: Vintage Decor for Today's Homes. Carole Coates & Annie Dietz. ISBN: 0764326356. $49.95

Decorator Show Houses. Tina Skinner, Melissa Cardona, & Nancy Ottino. ISBN: 0764320513. $44.95

Designer Showcase: Interior Design at its Best. Melissa Cardona and Nathaniel Wolfgang-Price. ISBN: 0764323989. $44.95

Inspired High-End Interior Design. Shane Reilly. ISBN: 0764324993. $44.95

Schiffer Books are available at special discounts for bulk purchases for sales promotions or premiums. Special editions, including personalized covers, corporate imprints, and excerpts can be created in large quantities for special needs. For more information contact the publisher:

Published by Schiffer Publishing Ltd.
4880 Lower Valley Road
Atglen, PA 19310
Phone: (610) 593-1777; Fax: (610) 593-2002
E-mail: Info@schifferbooks.com

For the largest selection of fine reference books on this and related subjects, please visit our web site at **www.schifferbooks.com**
We are always looking for people to write books on new and related subjects.
If you have an idea for a book please contact us at the above address.

This book may be purchased from the publisher.
Include $5.00 for shipping.
Please try your bookstore first.
You may write for a free catalog.

In Europe, Schiffer books are distributed by
Bushwood Books
6 Marksbury Ave.
Kew Gardens
Surrey TW9 4JF England
Phone: 44 (0) 20 8392 8585; Fax: 44 (0) 20 8392 9876
E-mail: info@bushwoodbooks.co.uk
Website: www.bushwoodbooks.co.uk

Copyright © 2009 by Schiffer Publishing, Ltd.
Library of Congress Control Number: 2009921121

Designed by RoS
Type set in University Roman Bd BT/Zurich BT

ISBN: 978-0-7643-3272-2
Printed in China

Contents

Introduction

Welcome to the land where interior designers play and leagues of volunteers toil – the Decorator Showhouse. These events are held around the nation, hosted by loyal volunteers dedicated to helping expand hospitals, fund public art organizations, sustain symphony orchestras, and raise funds for other noble causes.

A showhouse event is a monumental undertaking, requiring hundreds of volunteer man hours and buoyed upon boundless enthusiasm. The result is usually a historic home, repurposed for the cause, worked over by decorators and craftsmen, then trampled through by hordes for a few brief weeks before being disassembled and locked away from public view.

The purpose of this book is to preserve those noble efforts and, more than anything, to bring the creative genius and the endless ideas to the eyes of even more individuals. So if you haven't made it to one of Long Island's wonderful Mansions & Millionaire's showcase events, or traveled to the tip of the Jersey Shore for a Cape May classic, here's your opportunity for a glimpse. Showhouses from New England to California are featured, and the variety in between is astounding. Enjoy!

Chapter

1

Foyers & Hallways

Great Hall

Mansions & Millionaires Designers Showcase™
Baltimore Design Group
Ivy D Photography

A castle keep gets a dramatic update, with contemporary furnishings and splashes of bold color. Stone walls are summer-ized by garden colors.

A Seaside Corridor

Mansions & Millionaires Designers Showcase™
Catherine Deshler Interior Design
Ivy D Photography

Shimmering silk taffeta drapes and gilded frames add a Hollywood luster to this living space. Seashells encrust the chandelier and starfish add punctuation, and a reminder that this is a seaside escape.

Art Excursion
Cape May's Designer Showhouse
Pedro Rodriquez Interiors
Photography by John Armich

A sun porch gets an artful uplift with a geometric floor mural and funky black furnishings.

Parlor Room

Mansions & Millionaires Designers Showcase™
Billy Ceglia Designs, LLC
Ivy D Photography

A folding screen insulates an inside wall, adding castle motif to a space that would have been fitting for grand receptions in days gone by. Here it is partitioned into conversation pits and comfortable places to escape with a book.

Patterned Passage

Vanguard Designer Showhouse
Arthur Fowler of Charlton Studios
Randall Perry Photography

Reds and gold add warmth to a lengthy foyer, trimmed in rich woodwork. A repeating floor pattern is mirrored in wallpaper impressed with a foliage texture.

Cloistered Colonnade

**Jacksonville Symphony Guild-Designer
    Showhouse & Garden
Joanne Rumney of Design Loft Interiors
Photography by Bob Pearce of Chelsea Photographic**

A passageway gives pause, with pillowed benches that beckon one to stop and admire the day, or perhaps the fine lighting. An outdoor kitchen area provides sustenance, while the fireplace adds warmth to an evening gathering.

Forest Path
Vanguard Designer Showhouse
Jae Y. Schalekamp of MIN Studio
Photographer: Randall Perry

Wall murals imitate a waterfall and forest on this stair and landing, blending with muted colors on wall and window for a double-take effect. The cascading waterfall exudes the energy of motion, while falling leaves create an intimate and meditative mood.

Garden Entry
Lane Estate Showhouse
Eva & You Interior Design
Ivy D Photography

Latticework makes an entry foyer feel exterior, along with wicker furnishings.

Bud's Mud Room

Mansions & Millionaires Designers Showcase™
Regina T. Kraft
Pam Setchell of Viewpoint Photography

The Mudroom is the alpha and the omega of the home for today's active family and their guests. Not simply a repository for sporting equipment and outdoor gear, this space does double duty; The perfect place to perch to pull on your boots, or hang up your hat. The built in cabinetry elegantly conceals all the necessities of country life. In addition to the aforementioned functions, this room pays homage to man's best friend. His beautiful toile bed is in the perfect location to watch all the comings and goings of the other residents!

17

Rabbit-ed Joint

Vanguard Designer Showhouse
Nora Logan Studio
Photographer: Randall Perry

An Arts & Crafts era motif was hand-painted throughout a stairwell and landing, adding a sense of dimension and character to a confined space.

Jazz Age Hallway

Baltimore Symphony Decorator Showhouse
Pat O'Brien
Photographer: John J. Coyle Jr.

A hallway and stairs become a journey of nostalgia, with Art Deco graphics, a collection of original jazz age era poster art, and the uplifting zing of a brilliant peacock blue.

Inside Out

Mansion in May Showhouse
Nancy Marcus and Jim Guzman of
    Olcott Square Interiors
Photography by Emily Gilbert

A basement walkout area beckons, richly finished with carpeting and curtains. Lighting adds cheer to its stone and concrete confines, as do bright textiles.

Opulent Entry

Lane Estate Showhouse
M. Consolé Interiors
Ivy D Photography

Hand painted wallpaper originally installed by the famed Elsie de Wolfe 100 years ago set the tone for this designer. Aubusson silk and ormolu, does it get any better ...

Chapter

2

Studies & Libraries

Book Nook

Mansions & Millionaires Designers Showcase™
Billy Ceglia Designs, LLC
Ivy D Photography

Though a library might be dedicated to books, their mismatched covers needn't interfere with the peaceful studiousness of the room. White book covers and a numbering system can be used to make finding your reference book simple. The emphasis in this space is on comfort, with lots of pillows to make both floor and furniture more habitable for someone curling up with a book, and retractable lighting sheds illumination on text anywhere.

Tudor Tower

Mansions & Millionaires Designers
Showcase™
Billy Ceglia Designs, LLC
Ivy D Photography

A towering space is minimized with lighting, focusing the spotlight on where people sit and allowing the higher spaces to trail off along with stray thoughts. Leaded windows, herringbone floor, and paneled walls are accouterments that would impress in any room.

Feminine Reflections

Scarsdale Show House
diSalvo Interiors
Ivy D Photography

A feminine retreat was lavished with velvet, satin and sheers, shiny bits, and alluring rose hues. Textured wall panels in gold, outlined in cream, create contrast in burgundy walls.

Framed in Wood

Mansions & Millionaires Designers Showcase™
M. Consolé Interiors
Peter Kutcher Photography

Handsome woodwork created a canvas upon which this designer lavished golden textiles and favorite things. Custom artistry on the ceiling evokes the beauty of transitional weather, perhaps offering a break for ships fighting a storm above the mantel.

Study in Blue

The Designer Showhouse of New Jersey
Mannarino Designs, Inc.
Photography by Derek Wiesahahn

A home office doubles as a guest room. Some features in this small room are a built in corner unit, which works as a workstation and a place to display collectables; a leather club chair, which opens to a twin bed, and an ottoman with storage.

Studious Stop

Cape May's Designer Showhouse
Janis A. Schmidt of Dragonfly Interiors, LLC
John Armich Photography

A third-floor study celebrates its gambrel roofline. The ceiling was outlined in beams and accented in warm, textural fabrics. The low walls were finished in decorative tin. A sparkling chandelier adds life, as do faux ostrich leather seats. A third-floor study celebrates its gambrel roofline. The ceiling was outlined in beams and accented in warm, textural fabrics. The low walls were finished in decorative tin. A sparkling chandelier adds life, as do faux ostrich leather seats.

Stupendous Study

Junior League of Montclair Showhouse
Joel Woodard of Lichten Craig Architects LLP
Pieter Estersohn Photography

A faux tortoiseshell ceiling reflects a warm, earthy glow in this eclectic study, where antique and contemporary pieces are artfully married.

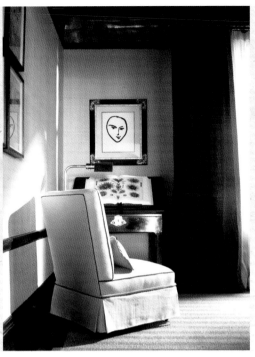

Gentleman's Clubhouse

Mansion in May Showhouse
William E. S. Kaufmann of WESKetch Architecture, Inc.
Emily Gilbert Photographer

Seclusion, sport, vintage wine, refuge ... a former smokehouse was converted to a gentleman's lair. A hunt room with a touch of sophistication, the rich plaster walls and heavy hand-hewn beams create a rustic place, timeless and simplistic.

Lofty Library

Saratoga Builders Association Showcase of Homes
Patricia DeMento and Stephen A. Momrow of Moose Creek Ltd.
Photography: Randall Perry

Tall, beamed ceilings and a hickory plank floor create a wonderful framework for this library, nestled atop a landing.

Ladies of Letters

Mansions & Millionaires Designers Showcase™
Susan Calabria of Noli Design Interiors
Ivy D Photography

A ladies writing room reflects a passion for finery and all things equine. Wood board and batten paneling forms a rich backdrop for generous, pooled draperies, a handsome carved desk, and a floral carpet underfoot.

Captain's Study
Cape May's Designer Showhouse
Michele and Bill Collins of Painted River Studios
John Armich Photography

This modern-day seafarer and world traveler has the pleasure of appreciating the original architecture of this 1847 house, transformed for twenty-first century living. Eclectic memorabilia from around the globe is organized in every nook and cranny. The 8 x 10-foot ceiling mural was executed in oil on canvas by Painted River Studios.

Chapter

3

Living Rooms

Vanilla Nice

Saratoga Showcase of Homes
Frank Barbera of Barbera Homes
Thomas R. Burns and Meghan Baltich of Blairhouse Interiors Group
Randall Perry Photographer

A bird's-eye view takes in the extent of a living area, furnished with comfortable roosts and illuminated by vanilla filters.

Private Seating

Vanguard Designer Showhouse
Mary Korzinski of Custom Design Associates and Patti Conners Interior Design
Decorative Painting by Mary Korzinski
Randall Perry Photography

Reed window screens preserve the privacy within while allowing half the sunlight from a bank of windows to illuminate the room. A mirror multiplies both the line and space. A geometric rose motif is repeated on wall and ceiling.

East Meets West
Mansions & Millionaires Designers Showcase™
diSalvo Interiors
Steve Geraci of Reflex Photo

Exotic art brings international flair to a dressed-to-impress living room. A crystal chandelier and pearly marble tones above reflect a sense of richness on formal, upholstered furnishings.

High Tech Inner Sanctum

Mansions & Millionaires Designers Showcase™
diSalvo Interiors
Ivy D Photography

Cubist art, modern motifs, and a neutral palette add a modern twist to a room paneled and molded in traditional dark wood. The dichotomy is alluring, and the casual addition of floor pillows before the fireplace invites instant relaxation.

Tudor Meets Hollywood Glam

Mansions & Millionaires Designers Showcase™
diSalvo Interiors
Ivy D Photography

Enormous leaded windows and a honeycombed ceiling helped dictate the formal nature of this room. White rugs, furnishings, and drapes lighten the effect of dark Tudor architecture.

Drawing on History

Merrywood, Greenwich Connecticut
diSalvo Interiors
Photographer: David R. Sloane

A period drawing room was outfitted in the style and grandeur traditional to a large well-appointed home. A contemporary color palate makes the space fresh and appealing for today's lifestyles.

Bright Clusters
NJ Designer Showhouse
Greg Lanza Design

Textile prints mix and add movement to a spacious sitting room. Conversation clusters are easily rearranged as gatherings dictate.

Parlor Craft

Cape May's Designer Showhouse
Terri Bell Matera of Carl Harz Furniture
John Armich Photography

In keeping with the craftsman style of the historic home where the Showhouse was held, a tapestry designed by William Morris creates a centerpiece over the brick fireplace and original Roseville pottery adorns the coffee table. Drawing on colors from Morris's palette, the room takes on the soft hues of a forest scene.

French Cottage Style

Cape May's Designer Showhouse
Terri Bell Matera of Carl Harz Furniture
John Armich Photography

The colors of Provence add cheerful delight to a great room, where dining and living intermingle. Window treatments are lightest of all, creating open invitation to welcome sunlight.

Warm Room

Cape May's Designer Showhouse
Mark D. Little of Design Home Interiors
Photography by John Armich

A tin ceiling reflects the warm, coppery tones of a plush, comfortable living room. Generous drapes soften a wall of windows and allow sunlight to be welcomed or warded off as the seasons dictate.

Stunning Sitting

Mansions & Millionaires Designers Showcase™
Judith Designs, Ltd.
Ivy D Photography

A marbled ceiling and textured walls create the backdrop for this dramatic sitting room, where blues and red punctuate the cream base.

Emerald Isle
Vanguard Designer Showhouse
Michel Patterson of Hudson River Fine Interiors
Photographer: Randall Perry

Kelly green walls lend a bright glow to a room grounded by rich, dark woodwork. These wood tones are echoed in the warm tones in the furnishings, the rich colors kept low to heighten the white ceiling and crown moulding.

Framed in Floral

Junior League of Greater Princeton Showhouse
Deborah Leamann Interiors
Photography by Tom Grimes

A casual linen floral textile frames this bay window, which has a magnificent view. A velvety window seat cushion is a great spot to curl up and enjoy the moment. This casual sitting room has a hand-painted desk and a lighted niche to display collections and mementos gathered from travels around the world.

Grand Salon

Atlanta Symphony Associates Decorators' Showhouse
Stephen Pararo and Nicole Burch Bachrach of
    Pineapple House Interior Design
Photography by Scott Moore

Unique furniture and artwork blend with classical architecture in this eclectic mix of styles and periods. Iron chandeliers suspend candlelights in keeping with the great castle halls of old.

Gilded Chamber

Junior League of Montclair Showhouse
Polo M.A., Inc.
Photographer: Peter Paige

A spectacular mix of tradition and today evokes opulence and romance while still addressing twenty-first century needs with LCD TV and internet access.

Butterfly Room

The Designer Showhouse of Saddle River, New Jersey
Eric J. Schmidt Interiors
Ivy D Photography

Winged specimens decorate the walls and mantel in a living room that balances the divide between ultra modern and cushy comfortable. Stainless steel stools in front of the fireplace reflect light and imprint the designer's initials.

Espalier Getaway

Junior League of Greater Princeton Showhouse
Totten-McGuirl Fine Interiors
Photographer: Paul S. Bartholomew

A repeated chinoiserie motif hand-painted over aqua stippled walls, compliment the cool sophistication of this 1930s inspired room.

That's Entertainment!

Hampton Designer Showhouse, New York
Shields & Company Interiors
Ivy D Photography

A Mongolian lamb antique French arm chair, a green and white Asian style ottoman, a unique chenille floor lamp, and snakeskin chairs once belonging to Pierre Cardin are among the eye-popping furnishings that compete with an eclectic collection of art and photography in this fashionable entertaining room.

Sand and Sky

Hampton Designer Showhouse, New York
Kate Singer Home
Ivy D Photography

*Patterns play in
a room, from the
framed print of skies,
to the carpeted
jumble of oblong
blocks. The playful
mix adds movement
to the room amidst
a palette of soft,
seaside tones.*

Sunny Disposition

Chilton Memorial Hospital Auxiliary House Tour
Tamara Dunner Interior Design
Photography by Peter Rymwid

Yellow sets a happy tone for a bright, lemony living room. Red accents, including red wall sconces and window blinds, add excitement.

Chapter

4

Sitting, Gathering, Keeping

The Rights of Spring Penthouse Lounge

Kips Bay Decorator Showhouse
Amy Lau Design
Photographer: Kris Tamburello

An imagination run wonderful, this space leaves you contemplating whether you're underwater or at the edge, with waves breaking over the couch and petals seeming to fall, or float, along a wall. Footstools add a minimal twist to the concept of pulling up a seat at the bar.

Zen Den

Mansions & Millionaires Designers Showcase™
Baltimore Design Group
Ivy D Photography

The Buddha brings serenity to a formal living room setting, where white tones subtly intermingle, punctuated by red ellipses. Birch wood sits ready for a bonfire in the expansive fireplace, and nature also finds its way into the room in the form of orchids, coral, and a pair of artful lovebirds.

Inner Sanctum

Mansions & Millionaires Designers Showcase™
Baron Goldstein Design Associates, Ltd.
Ivy D Photography

Lavender and Taupe set the mood in this modern sitting room. A sense of the historic home's 1920s Art Deco roots is maintained in mirror accents and stylized lines.

Deep Seating

Mansion in May Showhouse
Jeffrey B. Haines and Nancy Gentry
    of Butler's of Far Hills
Photography by Emily Gilbert

Thick carpet and a faux fur throw and soft chenille pillow – this is a sitting room you want to sink into.

Reclining Room

Mansions & Millionaires Designers Showcase™
Margreet Cevasco Design
Ivy D Photography

It's just a nook off the hallway, but one might easily find an afternoon slipping away here. A day bed by the window can be curtained off for daydreams, or a chaise lounge might invite a come hither pose that proves stress free. The rich tones of the wood floor are repeated in painted wall panels that contrast with the white, both in beautiful moulding and stylish furnishings.

Games People Play

Mansion in May Showhouse
Curren Design Associates
Emily Gilbert Photography

The card room was designed to accentuate the playful nature of the oval space. Perfect for poker, bridge, or just relaxing, the room is comfortable and fun yet still elegant. Each design element highlights the natural curvature of the room – from the hand-embossed ceiling to the rounded edges of the furniture. Soothing shades of green and chocolate suggest a fresh, botanical feel, while natural fabrics in silk, wool, and cotton create an environmentally friendly space.

Gentleman's Refuge
Mansion in May Showhouse
Daniel Mullay Interior Design and Decoration
Emily Gilbert Photography

Deep and delicious chocolate brown matte finished walls and crisp white trim create a masculine mood. A beautifully crafted Louis-Philippe style daybed is cushioned with lots of down and feather pillows for an afternoon nap or weekend stay. Chrome sconces add detail along with handsome floor lamps flanking the daybed and chair for reading light. Roman shades in men's wool suiting stripe dress the windows.

Victorian Parlor

Mansions & Millionaires Designers Showcase™
Dean Yoder Interiors, LLC
Ivy D Photography

Antiques and royal colors combine to recreate a drawing room of days gone by. Mirrors along one wall add a sense of depth to the long, narrow space.

Club Room

Merrywood, Greenwich Connecticut
diSalvo Interiors
Photographer: David R. Sloane

An intriguing dormer gets a clubby update, with bench seating and warm colors that beckon a small group to gather under the soaring ceiling.

Light Blue Parlor
Lane Estate Showhouse
diSalvo Interiors
Photographer: Steve Geraci Reflex Photo

A gilded ceiling reflects beautifully on decor fitting for a fourteenth century French Court. Blue and gold add color to white, keeping the room bright as befits a room outfitted with French doors.

Soft Landing

Mansions & Millionaires Designers Showcase™
Gerhard Designs
Ivy D Photography

A curtained seating area makes an attractive snuggle spot in this guest room with a day bed. Matching curtains and low-hung floral prints leave the high, sculpted white ceiling open for the imagination.

Modern Mix

Mansions & Millionaires Designers Showcase™
Greg Lanza Design

Wall panels by renowned artist Jose Maria Sert envelope a room with a sense of history. In their midst, modern furnishings contrast with an antique, carved rosewood chair.

Let Me Entertain You

Mansions & Millionaires Designers Showcase™
Jacqueline Ann Cappa, John Cappa and Francine
    Piazza of Piazza di Cappa
Ivy D Photography

A wet bar adds sparkle to any social occasion, and this comforting room lends itself to such encounters. Hunt country plaids and equestrian accouterments make the country set feel right at home.

Gallery Space

Mansions & Millionaires Designers Showcase™
Richard Schlesinger Interior Designs, Inc.
Ivy D Photography

A 1700s engraving of Paris adds interesting texture to a wall, while a coffered ceiling creates a sense of grand scale for the artful space.

Apartment Living Room

South Hampton Designer Showhouse
Rona Landman Interior Designs
Ivy D Photography

Jade lacquer tones leap out in an otherwise carefully understated room. Textile wall panels add classical flourish, picking up on the carpet motif featured in a framed photograph. A leopard skin rug and sleek modern furnishings belie classical embellishments, like busts and candelabra.

Hearth Room
Bellarmine Designers' Show House
Kevin Coleman and Marsha Riggle of Tassels & Tassels Too
Photographer: *Sophisticated Living Magazine* and
   Louisville Courier Journal

Rich reds and oranges interplay in a formal sitting room. Window treatments in three layers add a regal air.

Office Retreat
Mansions & Millionaires Designers Showcase™
Ziering Interiors
Ivy D Photography

A spacious closet has been converted to office space, with a wall mural of a bookcase providing added visual depth to the miniscule space. Wicker becomes regal in nearby seating, with satiny textile treatments.

Exotic Flair

Mansions & Millionaires Designers Showcase™
Jeani Ziering and Jennifer Huson of Ziering Interiors
Ivy D Photography

Golden tones warm a sunroom year round, with exotic flourishes like an animal print lamp, carved side chairs, and tropical wicker.

Kitchens

Espresso Kitchen
Cape May's Designer Showhouse
Rita Cipolla of Accessories Plus
John Armich Photography

Rich mocha tones impart an espresso flavor for this kitchen, building up from dark chocolate Brazilian wood flooring, mission-style Amaretto cream maple cabinetry, and java wood trim. Cream-colored stone tiles line the backsplash, underlined by a mix of marshmallow, walnut, and chocolate chip hues in the quartz countertop. Italian Murano glass pendant lights add atmosphere and aqua color. A mission-print pattern of cream, coffee, chocolate, and aqua dresses up the window areas to blend with the architectural style of the house. The state-of-the-art appliances blend in with an oiled bronze finish.

Old World Appeal

Mansions & Millionaires Designers Showcase™
Nava Slavin of The Creative Edge, Inc.
Ivy D Photography

A cobalt central island with an antiqued finish feels at home amidst antiqued walls that match the inlays in the existing old terracotta floor.

Cooking Arts and Crafts

Vanguard Designer Showhouse
Denise Maurer Interiors
Randall Perry Photography

Drawing on history, this kitchen serves up style in perfect keeping with the Arts and Crafts tradition. From the font over the entryway, to the patterned curtains and wood finish, this is very much a period kitchen. Cleverly, the designer has made much of little space by creating window seats that conceal radiators. Tiles behind the wet bar adorn a little nook well used to increase efficiency in the meal preparation. The handmade tile mural was first produced in 1997 for the Washington Square Public Library in Kalamazoo, Michigan. The Pines is a series of tile designed by Addison LeBoutittier and produced by Grueby Faience of Boston near the turn of the century

Earthy Modern
B.I.A. Parade of Homes
Dixon Designs
Photographer: Alanna Smith

This award winning kitchen features concrete countertops in dark greens, golds, and blacks. Over counter and under-counter lighting adds a warm glow to the cherry-stained cabinets. The backsplash consists of one-inch glass mosaic tiles of greens, browns, and ivory. The breakfast room features original artwork, and was created for comfort. Instead of the typical table surrounded by four chairs, this area features a sectional sofa, and lots of pillows for reclining, reading the paper, or just talking with the cook. The three tables are easily moved to configure to individual tables, or a large surface when placed together.

Warmed by Wood

Cape May's Designer Showhouse
Holloway Home Improvement Center, LLC
John Armich Photography

Wood tones permeate an expansive kitchen, lit by iron chandeliers and insulated by tile backsplashes and a tin ceiling. A marble floor creates a sense of history underfoot. Glass-fronted cabinets display beautiful serving ware, at hand for a casual meal at the expansive central island.

Barn Style Beauty

The Ardmore Free Library Annual
    Kitchen Tour Showhouse
The Stimmel Consulting Group, Inc
Photography by Charles Meacham

Nestled beneath a loft, a galley kitchen opens to the room beyond with barstool seating in barn style. Rustic woodwork on the cabinetry is in keeping with the country setting for this lovely space.

Working Kitchen
Orchard Hill Designer Showhouse
Regina T. Kraft
Pam Setchell of Viewpoint Photography

In the Butler's Pantry and adjoining kitchen, one sees the result of a sympathetic renovation rather than a complete renovation. State of the art appliances are juxtaposed with the clean and unfettered elements of a timeless functional workspace. The black and white tile floor reflects the past with a nod to the present with its bold, fresh look.

All Toile-d

The Ardmore Free Library Annual Kitchen Tour Showhouse
The Stimmel Consulting Group, Inc.
Photography by Charles Meacham

Pink toile fabric and walls make for a distinctive kitchen. This feminine touch is anchored by a stone floor and a stacked stone wall. An antique finish is the perfect complement to cabinetry pieces generously adorned with carved embellishments. It's easy to overlook the modern appliances, like wine coolers and warming trays, amidst all the finery.

Gracious Space

Chilton Memorial Hospital Auxiliary House Tour
Tamara Dunner Interior Design
Photography by Peter Rymwid

A kitchen becomes showplace in a classic presentation of fine cabinetry and granite countertops. Two islands assure plenty of space for food preparation, along with countertop seating next to the windowed breakfast nook.

Crystal & Cream

Charlotte Symphony Guild Showhouse
Teal Michel Interior Design
Photography: Dustin Peck

A pressed crystal chandelier makes a bold statement in this petite kitchen. Cream furnishings, from all cabinets to granite countertops, keep the effect soft, while dark under-counter cabinets anchor the room.

Breakfast in the Round

Mansions & Millionaires Designers Showcase™
Linda Rich of Willow of Locust Valley
Ivy D Photography

A circular breakfast nook gets floral flourishes, including a faux-painted wainscot that mimics massive wood balusters. Rattan furnishings keep the effect light and tropical.

Very Paris

Mansions & Millionaires Designers Showcase™
Vasi Ypsilantis of The Breakfast Room, Ltd.
Ivy D Photography

Louis XVI would have been proud to own this elaborate kitchen island, faced by elaborate veneer work and capped by handsomely veined marble. Its home, the kitchen, is an intriguing collection of antiqued cabinetry that evokes a sense of longevity for the room, seeming more a collection than a remodel.

Chapter

6

Dining Rooms

Sea Food

Mansions & Millionaires Designers Showcase™
Baltimore Design Group
Ivy D Photography

Natives are bringing in the feast in subtle shades of black and white on a quiet wall mural. Shells in all their studied beauty are used to adorn the room, from table decor to wall art.

Delightful Dining

Saratoga Showcase of Homes
Frank Barbera of Barbera Homes
Thomas R. Burns and Meghan Baltich of Blairhouse Interiors Group
Photographer: Randall Perry

Symmetry offers a sense of serenity to a small dining room. A bench seat helps save space and a spot to squeeze in that extra guest when the opportunity allows.

French Fancy
Mansions & Millionaires Designers Showcase™
Colleen Borek of Colleen Grace Designs
Ivy D Photography

A posh room is packed with feminine accents, from pink tassels and roses to multi-tiered crystals and silky textiles.

Attuned to Fine Tastes

Cape May's Designer Showhouse
Susan Stowell of Blue Chair Design Group
John Armich Photography

Fine furnishings and the opportunity for live entertainment make this dining room memorable. The table is set with deep blushes of burgundy, mirroring tones in a Moulin Rouge style painting and the border of a classic Oriental carpet.

Shining Dining

Mansion in May Showhouse
Frank DelleDonne Interiors, Inc.
Emily Gilbert Photography

This dining room was refinished and lightened to the warm color of toast. An oval rug on the floor creates interest and tension in the rectangular shaped dining room. The walls were papered in a handmade block print with a modern tree design. A large sunburst design of hand-painted tiles from Portugal highlights the back wall of the fireplace.

Feast for Five Senses

Mansions & Millionaires Designers Showcase™
diSalvo Interiors
Ivy D Photography

A dining room evokes baronial feasts of days gone by, with landed gentry recounting the day's outdoor pursuits. Wood paneling contributes to the room's intimate atmosphere, as do window treatments that create an indoor awning and a heightened sense of privacy.

Sophisticated Yet Warm

B.I.A. Parade of Homes
Dixon Designs
Photographer: Alanna Smith

Gold leaf on the chandelier and sconces in combination with shimmering silk window treatments evoke an aura of elegance in this dining room. At its center sits a round, zebrawood pedestal table with an impressive custom floral arrangement.

Toile Style
Orchard Hill Designer Showhouse
Joan Spiro Interiors
Ivy D Photography

Taking a cue from beloved collection of blue willow china, blue predominates. Die-cut wallpaper creates a lacy frame for this pretty blue breakfast nook, its toile pattern extending to the ceiling.

Carving the Meal

Cape May's Designer Showhouse
Terri Bell Matera of Carl Harz Furniture
John Armich Photography

Craftsman-era paneling and crown moulding dictated the clean lines for furnishing this open dining area. Stained glass and a tile mosaic recall the elegant legacy created during the early 1920s when this architectural beauty was created.

Lemon and Lime

Mansions & Millionaires Designers Showcase™
Katharine Jessica Interior Design LLC
Ivy D Photography

A fantasy pallet of citrus tones is intermingled in a sunny breakfast nook. Classic moulding, a chandelier, and wood flooring create a sense of place.

Everyday Treat
Chilton Memorial Hospital Auxiliary House Tour
Tamara Dunner Interior Design
Photography by Peter Rymwid

Candy striped curtains tone the appetite in a pretty dining room made bright by windows and a white recessed alcove.

The Garden Room

Junior League of Greater Princeton, New Jersey
Deborah Leamann Interiors
Photography by Tom Grimes

A gardener's paradise indoors, this charming breakfast room offers up foliage with refreshments. Antique ornithological and botanical prints enhance the walls. Lemony textiles create contrast. A banquette bench seat gets a creative cushion treatment, while flowering plant and whimsical wallpaper pull the space all together.

Power Lunches
Decorators' Showhouse
Umphrey Interiors
Photographer: Jeff White

Steel adds heft and import to stylish dining chairs, each armed and arranged around a round table.

Fresh Foods

Mansions & Millionaires Designers Showcase™
Linda Rich of Willow of Locust Valley
Decorative Painters: Sal and Nancy Moccia
Ivy D Photography

Decorative painting packs a few surprises into this spacious pantry, like a bird peaking in from the ceiling and fruit that's always fresh.

Chapter

7

Bedrooms

White Nights

Mansions & Millionaires Designers Showcase™
Isabelle L. Ferranti Interiors, Inc.
Ivy D Photographer

Femininity prevails in a room suffused with subtle pink hues and airy textiles. Crown moulding adds character to the space, and provides curtain pockets.

Safe Harbor

Mansions & Millionaires Designers Showcase™
Jackie Higgins of Beach Glass Designs
Ivy D Photography

A nautical theme is fitting for a historic home on Long Island. Shell specimens, a porthole mirror, and blue accents enhance the sense of a sailor's retreat.

Classic Garden Guest Bedroom

Cape May's Designer Showhouse
BMR Design Associates International
Photography by John Armich

A daybed and window seat, an enticing retreat, while accents create a sense of escape into a cottage garden.

Island Escape Bedroom
Cape May's Designer Showhouse
Nora Pascarella of Cape May Linen Outlet
Photography by John Armich

Broad floral strokes in textiles contribute to the tropical effect of an island-themed bedroom. Sunny walls and burnt orange accents highlight the soothing colors.

Draped Escape
Mansions & Millionaires Designers Showcase™
Colleen Borek of Colleen Grace Designs
Ivy D Photography

Textiles have been lavished on this guest bedroom, offering up layers of pink and green, gingham and florals.

Studied Studliness

Mansions & Millionaires Designers Showcase™
Kim E. Courtney Designs
Ivy D Photography

Handsome wood tone and an aura of establishment prevail in a room outfitted for a man of power and means. A massive fireplace and crown moulding above twelve-foot ceilings establish this suite as one of importance.

Her Heaven

Mansions & Millionaires Designers Showcase™
Mayo-Delucci Interiors
Ivy D Photography

Floral motifs make this room distinctively feminine. The inviting retreat includes a curved window seat, curtained bed, and pink and green patterns that are irresistibly charming.

Home Away
Cape May's Designer Showhouse
Mary Jo Gallaher of Greystone Interiors, LLC
John Armich Photography

A seaside cottage offers family and guests a comfortable place to unwind and relax, surrounded by the warmth of muted hues and classic fabrics. Treasured antiques and mementoes offer objects to contemplate while escaping daily cares.

Summer Slumber

Mansions & Millionaires Designers Showcase™
Joan Spiro Interiors
Ivy D Photography

A bay window seat is lavished with color, including yellow prints imported straight from the French countryside. Gingham walls add gaiety and an exotic light casts a soothing nighttime glow over all.

Deco Dreams

Mansions & Millionaires Designers Showcase™
Judith Designs, Ltd.
Ivy D Photography

Inspired by water views, this bedroom is immersed in pale blues and shimmering touches of silver. Curtains add a subtle delineation halfway through double hung windows.

Rosy Glow
Scarsdale Show House
Joan Spiro Interiors
Ivy D Photography

Red undertones add a feminine feel to a bedroom suite resplendent in golden hues. A blue, four-poster bed fits neatly into a curtained window nook. Faux painting on the other window creates a tree resplendent in foliage year round, and continues a lower level of painted panes that form a rest above the window seat.

Amber Alcove

Cape May's Designer Showhouse
Betsy King of Jupiter Dunes Designs
John Armich Photography

A welcoming respite on the third floor offers comfort under the eaves. Vintage luggage is packed with creature comforts, backed up by piles of pillows.

Stately Style
Saratoga Builders Association Showcase of Homes
Patricia DeMento and Stephen A. Momrow of Moose Creek Ltd.
Photography: Randall Perry

A leather quilt caps a bed furnished with faux furs, lit by leopard-shade lamps.

Master's Nest

Lane Estate Showhouse
Natalie Weinstein Design Associates
Photographer: Jack Ader

A nineteenth century residence is enhanced by the antique furniture, including a triple armoire and mahogany bed. An oversized oriental rug, hand-painted screen, and crystal chandelier (one of a pair in the room) adorn this 35-foot long master suite. Attention to detail is seen in every accessory, including the antique dog bed. The sitting area off the bath boasts a tranquil trompe l'oeil scene over the fireplace, which is flanked by a pair of antique gilt chairs. Soft colors and elegant silk fabrics help create a romantic yet tranquil setting.

Birchwood Bedroom

Cape May's Designer Showhouse
Michele and Bill Collins of Painted River Studios
John Armich Photography

A progressive movement, the Arts and Crafts style celebrated durability, simple forms, and functionality in opposition to the excesses of the Victorian era. This late nineteenth century sensibility was stepped up for the twenty-first century, updating the color palette for a fresher look with brighter greens, golds, and ambers. The traditional Craftsman-inspired natural frieze, or border, was exaggerated to become a full-size, hand-painted mural.

Padded Room

Mansions & Millionaires Designers Showcase™
Richard Schlesinger Interior Designs, Inc.
Ivy D Photography

A quilted headboard rises to the crown of flanking windows, while another window gets a padded underline in the form of a window seat. Lace curtains are embroidered with Chinese characters, in keeping with ancient Chinese art on the wall, and an aestheticism evocative of Asia.

Stress Addressed

Orchard Hill Showhouse
Kate Singer Home
Photography by Phillip Ennis

Muted tones erase stress in a spacious master suite. Framed sepia prints and subtle leaf-papered walls set the tone for the rest of the room.

Art Opening

Tucson Museum of Art Designer Showhouse
Lisa L. Reeves of Talents Design Studio, Inc.
Photographer: Tim Fuller

Textural wall surfaces and unique art pieces offer expanses to contemplate in a guest room furnished with daybeds.

Golden Goodnight
Vanguard Designer Showhouse
Terry L. Kral of Window Wear and Jeanie Masullo Interiors
Photographer: Randall Perry

A satin quilt carries on the tone of solid tan walls, a hue picked up in window treatments in an Arts & Crafts era theme.

Gleaming Getaway

Mansions & Millionaires Designers Showcase™
Ziering Interiors
Ivy D Photography

Lavender walls and a hydrangea quilt create a comfort zone of femininity. Gilded furnishings add gleam and glamour.

Chapter

8

Children's Bedrooms

Play Place

Lane Estate Showhouse
Esther Sadowsky of Charm & Whimsy
Photography: Tim Ebert

Accessible shelving, easily swept floor, and a door straight outdoors are factors that help a parent maintain sanity with young children.

De Bunk

Saratoga Builders Association Showcase of Homes
Patricia DeMento and Stephen A. Momrow of Moose Creek Ltd.
Photography: Randall Perry

This children's bedroom doubles as a favorite fort, with a rustic bunk bed and a lofty, tree-house sense of escape.

Bunny Burrow

Cape May's Designer Showhouse
Mary E.A Hudlow Dima of Daroo Designs
John Arm.ich Photography

Beatrix Potter inspired this dreamy nursery, nestled next to the master bedroom. A hand-painted mural embellished with gilding and glass beads adds texture and dimension that bring this magical room to life. The faux marquetry valance is stained to give the illusion of inlaid wood. A soft combination of beautiful satins fill the crib and cover the windows, wrapping the room in subtle warmth.

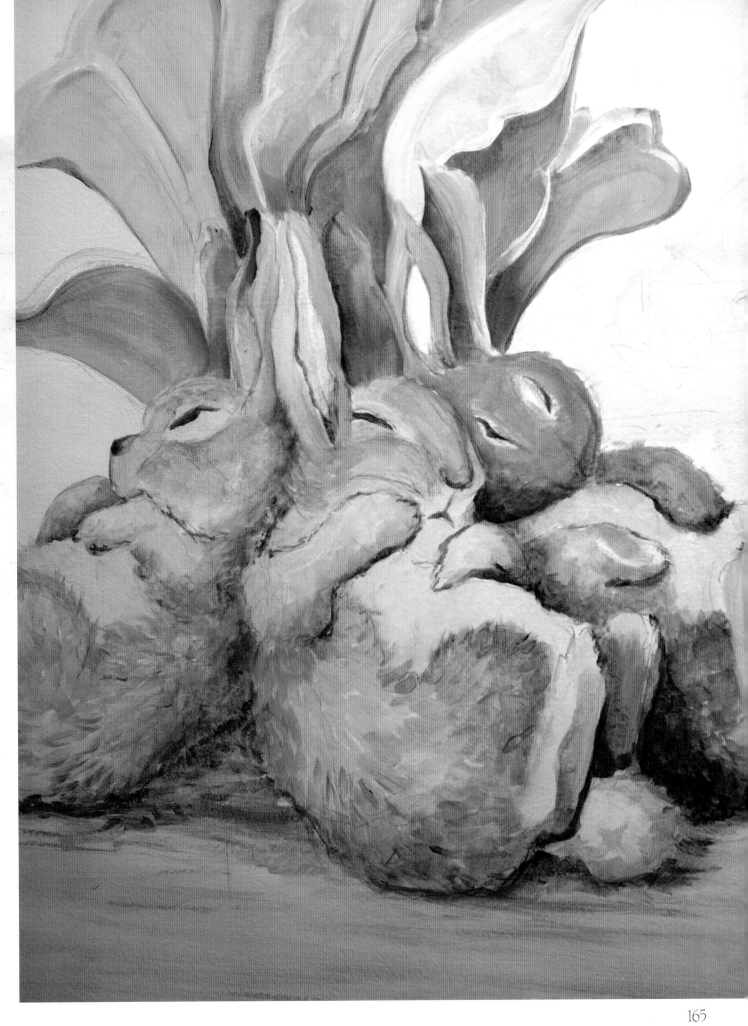

Little Girl's Garden

Cape May's Designer Showhouse
Mary EA Hudlow Dima of Daroo Designs
Photography by John Armich

This special room is the perfect retreat for a young girl. With a garden mural that wraps around the wall and ceiling, this delightful room brings the tranquil outdoors in. Hand-painted furniture, a painted floor cloth, and a custom clock add to the charm of this peaceful haven, designed especially for reading and relaxing. Even if it's raining outdoors, she'll awake each day to a bright new beginning!

Slumberland in Wonderland
Cape May's Designer Showhouse
LouLou of Lou Lou's Whimsicals
John Armich Photography

Look out Alice, the mushroom on the left makes you grown. A little girl's room is all set for a tea party, but it looks like the white rabbit is late.

Fairytale Tower

Mansions & Millionaires Designers Showcase™
Inspired Style Designs Michele, Kowalski Interiors
Ivy D Photography

*A **true** princess lies happily ensconced in this frilly room, furnished to foster fantasy.*

Baby and Me
Mansions & Millionaires Designers Showcase™
Susan Calabria of Noli Design Interiors
Ivy D Photography

Pinks and greens grace a sweet nursery, providing a private little getaway for mother and child.

Chapter

9

Bathrooms

Tiled Treat

Cape May's Designer Showhouse
Avalon Carpet Tile and Flooring
John Armich Photography

Italian porcelain tile in warm and comfortable tones, such as caramel with an accent of copper glass, adds a European feel to this third-floor bath. The addition of a traditional sink chest in a subtle two-tone effect coordinates perfectly with the color palette.

Moroccan Fantasy
Cape May's Designer Showhouse
Michael Byrne Painting, Inc.
John Armich Photography

To fit in to its historic Arts & Crafts era home, the designer interpreted the Morris tradition of adopting a medieval or esoteric theme. Beaded trim and embroidered fabric creates a Middle Eastern feel. The carved wood bench was fitted with a satin sea blue cushion layered with pillows rich in beads and trims, and a crystal-cut sconce was set into the mirror. The ceiling was faux finished in swirling red tones atop the golden walls.

Exhilarating Beginnings
Mansion in May Showhouse
Karla Trincanello for Interior Decisions, Inc.
Photography: by Peter Rymwid

Wave motifs in tile mosaic repeat throughout the bath, their subtle colors creating a frame for a mirror, a pedestal for a soaking tub, and a backsplash for the his and hers vanity. The walls are hand-painted in a Strie style and then silver leaf "rain" drops give that fresh feeling of a summer shower.

Bath Time

Lane Estate Showhouse
Esther Sadowsky of Charm & Whimsy
Photography: Tim Ebert

Anyone who has raised kids knows that hygiene is only secondary to what goes on during bath time. This room was outfitted with the love and care of a parent who knows that kids just want to have fun. No one is going to holler about the walls getting wet in this room. Nor will a splatter of toothpaste destroy this special space.

Crystal Clean

Mansions & Millionaires Designers Showcase™
McNeill Design Consultants Corp.
Ivy D Photography

Crystals were lavished on chandelier and sconces that illuminate a glowing bath. Draperies soften the room and add a sense of lingering luxury.

Crystal Bath

Lane Estate Showhouse
Lori Miller of Lori-Girl Creations, Inc.
Photography by Ken Hild Photographers

Satiny walls with pink roses reflect the glow from the crystal-clad lighting that adorns this feminine bath. Contrasting green and gold focuses an architectural eye on the wainscoting and door.

Second Floor Hall Bath

Cape May's Designer Showhouse
MJ Designs
John Armich Photography

The faux walls of a soft peach with a metallic copper overlay welcomes you with a feeling of earthly warmth to this bathroom retreat. The imported soft natural hue of the Italian porcelain tiles with Laguna/ gold/copper glass accents on the floor envelope the visitor. Brass and bronze vanity, shower and tub fixtures along with the bronze lighting fixtures compliment the earth tones of the room. The warm mahogany of the double bowl vanity allows a couple to simultaneously enjoy this retreat.

Family Bath

Vanguard Designer Showhouse
Moore Interior Designs
Photographer: Randall Perry

A bath includes a foot bath which takes on a "new life" for a beloved Cairn terrier.

The Mistress' Bath

The Designer Showhouse of New Jersey
M.R. Sferra Interior Design
Photography: Peter Rymwid

The aura of Pompeii is recreated in this luxurious retreat. Faux painted panels define the octagonal stepped ceiling, crowned by a dramatic tented silk medallion. Palladian windows with paintings of antiquity inserts, subtle draped window treatment, and fresco-like walls, provide the perfect backdrop for the marble platform whirlpool bath. Centered atop a patterned mosaic, a bronze caryatid stand offers a selection of towels.

Full Bath with Punch

Orchard Hill Showhouse
Kate Singer Home
Photography by Phillip Ennis

A mirror under the window adds space to a tight master bath setting, and purple adds punctuation.

Chapter

10

Special Purpose Spaces

Quilts & Crafts Room

Junior League of Montclair Showhouse
Diane Boyer Interiors, LLC
Photography by Phillip Ennis

An attic craft room creates a colorful place to escape and be creative. Custom maple cabinets house books and supplies, and there are specially designed areas for sewing, scrapbooking, gift-wrapping, and general crafting. A television over the fireplace adds entertainment for an owner who wants to sit and knit, and there's plenty of room for family members to share in the magic of creating something special.

Whimsy and Wow
Lane Estate Showhouse
Esther Sadowsky of Charm & Whimsy
Photography: Tim Ebert

Butterfly chairs and paper lanterns add charm to a porch, as do two additions of fresh sod. A hammock embodies the ultimate in tropical escape fantasies.

Second Floor Porch

Cape May's Designer Showhouse
Nora Pascarella of Cape May Linen Outlet
Photography by John Armich

A second floor porch is a private paradise with upholstered furniture and pillows, and curtains that can be drawn to screen out sun, or prying eyes

Game Time
Cape May's Designer Showhouse
Linda Daly of Interior Outlook
Photography by John Armich

It's all fun and games in this attic getaway, where a garden of model trains circles billiard and poker tables in a Mark Twain themed room. The result is a getaway easily fit for one to twenty.

Beauty Blooms

Mansion in May Showhouse
Vanessa DeLeon Associates
Decorative Painter: Mike Goldberg of Classic Décor, New Jersey
Dan Muro of Fast Forward Unlimited

A glamorous dressing room provides a two-tone backdrop of beauty rituals. The decorative painter picked up on the border in a rug pattern to make like flowers bloom on the walls. A faux finish on the ceiling is another subtle touch that keeps the focus on the beauty within.

Dressing Suite with Shoe Pagoda

National Symphony Orchestra Celebrations: Beyond Dragons:
   An East-West Fusion of Interior Design
Janet Morais, and Anna Beck Bimba, of DeMorais & Associates, PLLC

Eastern exoticism meets Western elegance in this dramatic ladies dressing suite. A true shoe lover's dream is a temple in which to display and admire their prized possessions! An Asian inspired glass encased shoe pagoda serves not only as an amazing display for a shoe collection but also as a work of art, and a black lacquer dresser contrasts beautifully with raspberry and gold accents.

Distinctive Wine

Cape May's Designer Showhouse
Vera Bahou of Designhaus Interiors
John Armich Photography

Craftsman-style architecture got an artistic update in a modern wine bar area. Colorful onyx fronts a swoosh of bar and the backdrop for a display area.

Room for Wellness
Cape May's Designer Showhouse
Vera Bahou of Designhaus Interiors
Photography by John Armich

Laundry facilities are de-emphasized in a space dedicated to wellness. Room for exercise and an area dedicated to massage and relaxation are paramount, while a shower serves a convenient fresh-up function after exertion or oiling.

Bride's Dressing Room
Mansions & Millionaires Designers Showcase™
Kim E. Courtney Interiors
Ivy D Photography

Ivory tones act as the perfect backdrop for a white gown and blushing bride as she gathers with those nearest and dearest to prepare for the ultimate event.

Linger-longer Loggia
Mansions & Millionaires Designers Showcase™
Giovanni Naso Designs
Ivy D Photography

Curtains and furnished alcoves in an extensive loggia create an invitation to stay. The garden creeps in as well, with potted plants and paintings of pastoral scenes.

Shelterless Splendor

Mansions & Millionaires Designers Showcase™
Giovanni Cipriano
Ivy D Photography

A rustic pergola creates a framework for an intimate outdoor patio warmed by fire. Blue glass brings color to the setting, creating a fascinating pallet in slate planters.

Civilized Outlook

St. Matthews Episcopal Day School Dickens House
Christian Huebner Interiors, Inc.
Photographer: Susan Munroe

An eighteenth century Italian screen from the late landscape designer Tommy Church marks the periphery of a terrace. Wicker gets a contemporary twist in straight-lined, upholstered furnishings.

Musically Inclined

Lane Estate Showhouse
Geanine Palmer and Kathy Rayfield of PYW Interiors
Decorative Painter: Monique

A music room directly off of the reception foyer was endowed with a rounded tray ceiling. This was embellished with a dramatic faux autumn sky, and toile-like cameos of hand-painted musical instruments. Metallic wall coverings emulate antique mirrors inside panels and surrounded it with an unexpected horizontal ribbed paper that you couldn't help but touch. The furniture is classic, while the fabrics are contemporary in rich printed silks and animal patterned cut velvet.

Cinematic Magic

Stately Homes by the Sea Designer Showhouse
Karla Trincanello of Interior Decisions, Inc.
Photography: Marisa Pellegrini

Rich plum tones and golden accents bring the magic of Hollywood into a home theater. The tiered ceiling rises to a compass medallion, reminiscent of the great theatrical venues of old. A bar in the foyer serves up libations found only in the finest of establishments.

Essential Indulgence
Cape May's Designer Showhouse
Joseph Design, LLC
John Armich Photography

A wine cellar becomes a privileged dining hall for those closest to the keeper. A tiled passageway under a vaulted brick ceiling, a curtained room, and rich, dark woodwork lend themselves to the sense of going back in time, to a baron's castle keep.

Indulgence Continued
Cape May's Designer Showhouse
Joseph Design, LLC
John Armich Photography

Happiness and good times were uppermost in the plans for this media room. Faux finishes and eclectic furnishings are among the entertainments, interposed with cozy pillows and ottomans. Storage space makes this a stash spot for life's little extras, while the room works as a space to escape cares.

Treillage Room

Lane Estate Showhouse
Garden Schemes and Leighton & Associates Design Services
Photography by Vinnie Fish

The designers reinterpreted one of the few surviving treillage rooms installed by Elsie de Wolfe, attempting to capture her spirit of informality and eclecticism. The conservatory or trellis room was popular during the 1890-1920s, and was referred to as the "Winter Garden Room." These rooms often combined French furniture, Chinese antiques, garden statuary, Oriental carpets, and collections of specimen plants. Here the lady of the house could relax and receive guests for tea in a less formal, but still luxurious, atmosphere.

Bridal Array

The Stately Homes by the Sea, Rumson, New Jersey
Mannarino Designs, Inc.
Photography by Wing Wong

A bride's corner awaits the special day, when dearest maids and mothers will confer in a busy rush of tradition and anticipation.

Fiery Porch

Saratoga Builders Association Showcase of Homes
Patricia DeMento and Stephen A. Momrow of Moose Creek Ltd.
Photography: Randall Perry

A massive stone chimney dominates a lofty porch room. Black wicker furniture upholstered in bold stripes makes its point within the intimate, screened setting.

Smoking Parlor

Mansions & Millionaires Designers Showcase™
Susan Calabria of Noli Design Interiors
Ivy D Photography

An old-fashioned men's study creates an atmosphere for gaming, from billiards and cards to a chess table by the window.

Crafty Games
Cape May's Designer Showhouse
Mark D. Little & Dominique Brouillard of Design Home Interiors
John Armich Photography

Immerse yourself in a sea of sandy neutrals in a modern interpretation of the Craftsman style. Rich, dark woods anchor the geometric patterns and organic taupe hues of the down-filled sectional. Cuddled by elegant sconces, this sanctuary provides comfortable ambience for visiting family and friends. Crisp accents in vibrant green provide a playful environment in which to be entertained.

The Crush

Twin Maples Centennial Showhouse
NLM Designs
Photographer Marisa Pellegrini

The rear and side walls feature maple cabinetry stained evoking the look of an aged mahogany. The cabinets were designed with lit niches paneled and antiqued glass for storage and display of over 225 wine bottles. A Tiffany stained glass transom graces the entry of the room and directly ahead, a rear lit window centered in the cabinet wall gives the impression that one is on street level and features a custom designed 'faux' wrought iron grate made from recycled materials. A four-paneled door depicting the harvest and crush of grapes was one of custom designed pieces for this room. A unique wine server was created with a slab of reclaimed redwood and re-purposed hickory bourbon barrels pull up to a cherry tasting table.

Glamorous Woman's Retreat

Mansions & Millionaires Designers Showcase™
M. Consolé Interiors
Ivy D Photography

A dreamy nook, furnished in willowy fabrics, mirrored furnishings, and sculpted carpeting was created as a feminine escape.

Gentleman's Dressing Room

Mansions & Millionaires Designers Showcase™
Sheila Rich Interiors
Photography by Wing Wong

A Seville Row atmosphere imbues a gentleman's room while keeping it warm and welcoming with rich textured wallpaper and a coordinated window treatment. The dark, wood planked floor is warmed by an area rug. These colors of nature also reflect the gentleman's interest in outdoor activities.

Chapter

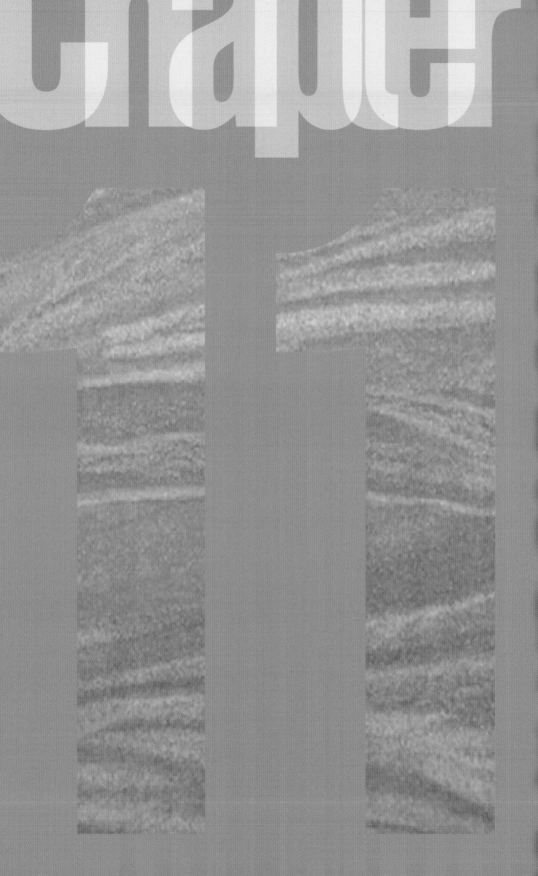

Master Suites

Golden Suite

Mansions & Millionaires Designers Showcase™
Angela Richards of Timeless Design Interiors
Ivy D Photography

Soothing tones gild this guest suite. Golden toile prints paper both bed and bath, and shimmering curtains cocoon this inviting nest.

White Nights
Mansions & Millionaires Designers Showcase™
Billy Ceglia Designs, LLC
Ivy D Photography

Shag carpeting is the perfect under-foot tonic for draining away a day's stress. Pristine whites and soothing beige add to the invitation of this relaxing, restful retreat.

Wide Window
Mansions & Millionaires Designers Showcase™
diSalvo Interiors
Photographer: Steve Geraci Reflex Photo

Neutral tones blend for a restful atmosphere in a sun-soaked master bedroom. Window treatments would have been a crime given the ornate moulding that adorns the wonderful picture window.

Crowning Glory

Mansions & Millionaires Designers Showcase™
diSalvo Interiors
Ivy D Photography

Royal touches—a crowning valance over the bed, a crystal chandelier, gilded art, and satin pillows mark this room as one fit for royalty.

Plastic Fantastic
Orchard Hill Designer Showhouse
Greg Lanza Design

Laminate finishes, chrome, and glass add modern impact to a bedroom suite.

Royal Repose
Cape May's Designer Showhouse
Janis A. Schmidt of Dragonfly Interiors, LLC
Photography by John Armich

Lush fabrics and gilded tones against a base of oh-so-civilized light blues bring a sense of French aristocracy to this master bedroom. A big budget of passamenterie makes windows and pillows resplendent. Even the ceiling got texture and pizzazz with a gilded paper that is repeated in silver and blue in the master bath.

Subtle Suite

St. Matthews Episcopal Day School Dickens House
Christian Huebner Interiors, Inc.
Photographer: Susan Munroe

Muted tones induce relaxation in a master suite. A painting on the wall creates texture, as does an upholstered, built-in headboard surround that absorbs sound and creates a sense of soundproof protection. The muted earth tones carry through to the master bath, repeated in marble tile and countertop.

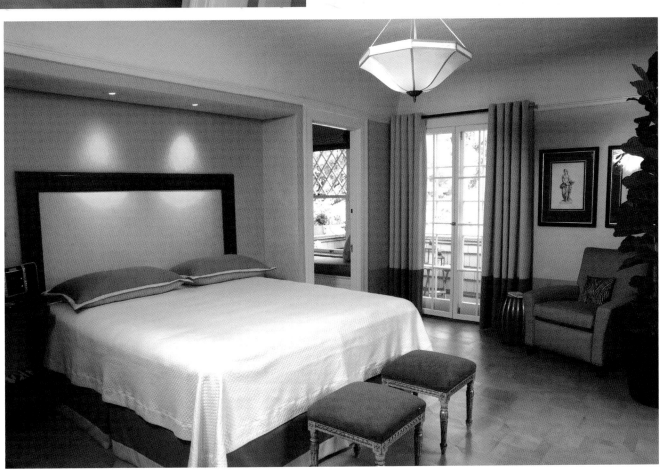

Jackie's Retreat

Stately Homes by the Sea Designer Showhouse
Karla Trincanello for Interior Decisions, Inc.
Photography: Peter Rymwid

A royal retreat tucked under the eaves offers a stately getaway. Within molding frames, a hand-painted, silver-toned diamond pattern adds a sheen to the setting, working in unison with carefully selected satin and velvet textiles. The lavishness of those textiles creates a cocooned escape, with nooks in dormer windows, and curtains to seal off private places like the dressing room that was created by adding a wall to square off the space for the bedroom area.

White on White

Cape May's Designer Showhouse
Jacqueline's Interior Design Studio, Inc.
John Armich Photography

At the end of a busy day at the shore, whether it was spent boating, sunning, entertaining, or antiquing, the host and hostess of this beautiful historic home have earned the right to "float" to sleep. A master bedroom offers blissful white comfort, along with art to contemplate.

Master Bedroom
Cape May's Designer Showhouse
Grace Kelly Designs
John Armich Photography

Faux painting continues the rock motif from the fireplace, and adds flourish to a headboard. A breakfast nook provides a private tea-for-two meeting spot.

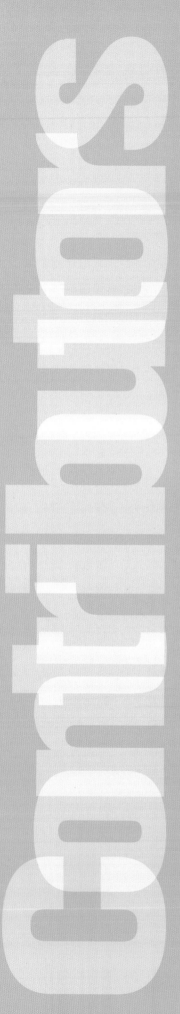

Designers

Accessories Plus
Sewell, New Jersey
856-374-8116

Aman & Carson
New York, New York
www.amancarson.com

Amy Lau Design
New York, New York
www.amylaudesign.com

Avalon Carpet Tile and Flooring
Rio Grande, New Jersey
www.avaloncarpettile.com

Baltimore Design Group
Port Washington, New York
www.baltimoredesigncenter.com

Barbera Homes
Albany, New York
www.barberahomes.com

Baron-Goldstein Design Associates,
Ltd.
Roslyn, New York
www.barongoldsteindesign.com

Beach Glass Designs
Huntington Bay, New York
www.beachglassinteriordesigns.com

Billy Ceglia Designs, LLC
Sandy Hook, Connecticut
www.billyceglia.com

Blairhouse Interiors Group
Newtonville, New York
www.blairhouseinteriors.com

Blue Chair Design Group, LLC
Newtown Square, Pennsylvania
www.bluechairdesigngroup.com

BMR Design Associates International
Mullica Hill, New Jersey
www.BMRDesigner.net

The Breakfast Room, Ltd.
Manhasset, New York
www.thebreakfastroom.com

Butler's of Far Hills
Far Hills, New Jersey
www.butlersoffarhills.com

Cape May Linen Outlet
Cape May, New Jersey
www.capemaylinen.com

Carl Harz Furniture
Elmer, New Jersey
www.carlharzfurniture.com

Catherine Deshler Interior Design
Patchogue, New York
516-978-2840

Charlton Studios
Ballston Lake, New York
www.awfowler.com

Charm & Whimsy
New York City, New York
www.charmandwhimsy.com

Christian Huebner Interiors, Inc.
www.huebnerinteriors.com
650-558-8700

Colleen Grace Designs
Hartsdale, New York
914-949-1975

The Creative Edge, Inc.
Roslyn Heights, New York
www.thecreativeedgeinc.com

Curren Design Associates
Mendham, New Jersey
973-543-3700

Custom Design Associates
Clifton Park, New York
www.customdesignassociates.com

Daniel Mullay Interior Design and Decoration
Chatham, New Jersey
973-701-2001

Daroo Designs
Blue Bell, Pennsylvania
www.daroodesigns.com

Dean Yoder Interiors, LLC
Glen Cove, New York
www.deanyoderinteriors.com

Deborah Leamann Interiors
www.deborahleamanninteriors.com
609-737-3330

DeMorais & Associates, PLLC
Old Town Manassas, Virginia
www.demoraisid.com

Denise Maurer Interiors
Troy, New York
www.denisemaurerinteriors.com

Design Home Interiors
www.designhomeinteriors.org
215-361-9100

Design Loft Interiors
Jacksonville, Florida
904-288-6699

Designhaus Interiors
New Holland, Pennsylvania
www.designhausinteriors.net

Diane Boyer Interiors, LLC
Verona, New Jersey
www.dianeboyerinteriors.com

diSalvo Interiors
New York, New York
www.disalvointeriors.com

Dixon Designs
Powell, Ohio
www.MaryDixonDesigns.com

Dragonfly Interiors, LLC
Cape May, New Jersey
www.DragonflyInteriorsLLC.com

Eric J. Schmidt Interiors
www.ericschmidtinteriors.com
212-288-3431

Eva & You Interior Design
Port Jefferson, New York
www.evaandyou.com

Frank DelleDonne Interiors, Inc.
Summit, New Jersey
908-598-1670

Garden Schemes
www.gardenschemes.com
631-584-4545

Gerhard Designs
Islip, New York
631-807-7410

Giovanni Cipriano
Port Jefferson, New York
516-903-7251

Giovanni Naso Designs
Bellport, New York
www.giovanninasodesigns.com

Grace Kelly Designs
Wildwood, New Jersey
609-846-1705

Greg Lanza Design
New York, New York
www.greglanza.com

Greystone Interiors, LLC
Haddonfield, New Jersey
856-429-6233

Holloway Home Improvement Center, LLC
Marmora, New Jersey
www.hollowayhomeimprovement.com

Home & Garden / Eva & You Interior Design
Port Jefferson, New York
www.evaandyou.com

Hudson River Fine Interiors
Loudonville, New York
www.HudsonRiverFineInteriors.com

Inspired Illusions by Monique
631-239-6382
www.inspiredillusionsbymonique.com

Inspired Style Designs/Michele Kowalski Interiors
Manorville, New York
631-871-0835

Interior Decisions, Inc.
Karla Trincanello
973-765-9013
www.interiordecisions.com

Interior Outlook
Ivyland, Pennsylvania
www.interioroutlook.com

Isabelle L. Ferranti Interiors, Inc.
Huntington, New York
631-871-0835

Jacqueline's Interior Design Studio, Inc.
Cherry Hill, New Jersey
856-424-9998

Jeanie Masullo Interiors
Voorheesville, New York
518-765-2594

Joan Spiro Interiors
Great Neck, New York
516-829-9087

Joseph Design, LLC
www.josephdesignllc.com
609-972-3477

Judith Designs, Ltd.
www.judithdesignsltd.com
516-621-1218

Jupiter Dunes Designs
Ocean City, New Jersey
609-398-8824

Kate Singer Home
www.katesingerhome.com
631-261-8376

Katharine Jessica Interior Design LLC
www.kj-id.com
631-418-8491

Kim E. Courtney Interiors
Muttontown, New York
www.ecourtneyinteriors.com

Leighton & Associates Design Services
www.LeightonAndAssociates.com
631-584-3011

Lichten Craig Architects LLP
www.lichtencraig.com
212-229-0200

Lori-Girl Creations, Inc.
www.lorigirlcreations.com
516-317-9083

Lou Lou's Whimsicals
www.LouLousWhimsicals.com
484-680-4487

M. Consolé Interiors
Northport, New York
631-757-0002

M.R. Sferra Interior Design
www.mrsferrainteriordesign.com
201-384-8965

Mannarino Designs, Inc.
www.mannarinodesigns.com
732-741-1444

Margreet Cevasco Design
Sea Cliff, New York
www.margreetcevascodesign.com

Mason Barrister, Inc.
Livingston, New Jersey
973-740-9233

Mayo-Delucci Interiors
New York, New York
212-752-2762

McNeill Design Consultants Corp.
www.McNeillinteriors.com
631-219-2905

Michael Byrne Painting, Inc.
Flourtown, Pennsylvania
www.MichaelByrnePainting.com

MIN Studio
www.2minstudio.com
518-892-5178

MJ Designs
Cape May Court House, New Jersey
609-425-3135

Moore Interior Designs
Cohoes, New York
www.mooreinteriordesigns.com.

Moose Creek Ltd.
www.moosecreekltd.com
518-869-0049

Natalie Weinstein Design Associates
St. James, New York
631-862-6198

NLM Designs
www.nlmdesigns.net
973-241-5151

Noli Design Interiors
www.nolidesigninteriors.com
516-609-9065

Nora Logan Studio
www.noraloganstudio.blogspot.com
518-797-3243

Olcott Square Interiors
www.olcottsquareinteriors.com
908-696-8000

Painted River Studios
www.PaintedRiverStudios.com
609-628-4564

Paper Your World Interiors
Miller Place, New York
631-209-1500

Pat O'Brien
www.bestmuralist.com
410-303-0233

Patti Connors Interior Design
Mechanicville, New York
518-664-1616

Pedro Rodriquez Interiors
Bala Cynwyd, Pennsylvania
610-660-9611

Piazza di Cappa
Locust Valley, New York
516-676-0760

Pineapple House Interior Design
www.pineapplehouse.com
404-897-5551

Polo M.A., Inc.
www.polomainc.com
973-402-7400

PYW Interiors
Miller Place, New York
631-209-1500

Regina T. Kraft
Interior Design and Consultation
Cold Springs Harbor, New York
631-692-6278

Richard Schlesinger Interior Designs, Inc.
New York, New York
212-513-7977

Rona Landman Interior Design
www.ronalandmaninteriordesign.com
212-996-8171

Sheila Rich Interiors, LLC
www.sheilarichinteriors.com
732-870-3012

Shields & Company Interiors
www.shieldsinteriors.com
212-679-9130

The Stimmel Consulting Group, Inc.
www.stimmeldesign.com
215-542-0772

Talents Design Studio, Inc.
Tucson, Arizona
520-326-1172

Tamara Dunner Interior Design
www.tamarasinteriors.com
973-951-8908

Tassels & Tassels Too
Louisville, Kentucky
502-245-7887

Teal Michel ASID Interior Design
www.tealmichelasid.com
704-554-7035

Timeless Design Interiors
Lloyd Harbor, New York
631-425-1288

Totten-McGuirl Fine Interiors
www.totten-mcguirl.com
908-580-9572

Umphrey Interiors
Birmingham, Alabama
205-422-6969

Vanessa DeLeon Associates
Edgewater, New Jersey
www.vanessadeleon.com

WESKetch Architecture, Inc. and
WESK Interiors, Inc.
www.wesketch.com
908-647-8200

Willow of Locust Valley
Locust Valley, New York
516-674-9628,

Window Wear
www.WindowWearEtc.com
518-355-0063

Ziering Interiors
www.zieringinteriors.com
516-869-1049

Showhouses

Atlanta Decorators' Showhouse –
www.decoratorsshowhouse.org/
3750 Tuxedo Road, Camelot. 404-733-4935

Ardmore Free Library Annual Kitchen Tour
Showhouse
This event is held annually to raise funds for
the library as well as charitable events within
the community.

Baltimore Symphony Decorator Show House –
www.bsomusic.org
For more than three decades, the Baltimore
Symphony Associates has presented this
annual fundraiser to benefit the symphony's
educational programs. The city's leading designers are showcased.

Bellarmine Designers' Show House –
www.bellarmine.edu
The Manor House at Glenview Springs 6005
Springhouse Farm Lane Louisville, Kentucky

BIA Parade of Homes
The Building Industry Association of Central
Ohio represents single and multiple family
homebuilders, developers, and remodelers
in the area. Other members include subcontractors, suppliers, and service professionals.
Founded in 1943, its primary services include
legislative and regulatory representation, de-
velopment of favorable public perceptions of
the industry, promotion of business standards,
and support of homeownership. The BIA is the
annual sponsor of the Parade of Homes, Con-
do Quest, and the Showcase of Remodeled
Homes. BIA, 495 Executive Campus Drive,
Westerville, Ohio 43082. 614-891-0575, James
B. Hilz, Executive Director.

Cape May's Designer Showhouse –
www.capemay.org.
This charming coastal town has drawn thousands to its annual decorator showhouses
since 2004. Proceeds benefit the Mid-Atlantic
Center for the Arts, an organization that pro-

motes and preserves area history, provides on-
going restoration of the Emlen Physick Estate,
the Lighthouse, and other regional landmarks,
and encourages the performing arts. Contact:
Margo Harvey, fax: 609-884-0574, mharvey@
capemay.org

Charlotte Symphony Guild ASID Showhouse –
www.symphonyguildcharlotte.org
This event raises funds for the Charlotte Symphony Orchestra and youth music education
programs. Phone: 704-525-0522, email: of-
fice@symphonyguildcharlotte.org

Chilton Memorial Hospital Auxiliary House
Tour
Every two years for over thirty years, the
Smoke Rise gated community in Kinnelon,
New Jersey, has been home to the Chilton Me-
morial Hospital Auxiliary House Tour. This spe-
cial event has raised hundreds of thousands of
dollars for the hospital.

Decorators' Showhouse –
www.symphonyvolunteercouncil.org
The first Decorators' ShowHouse in support of
the Alabama Symphony Orchestra was held in
1976. Since that time, the volunteer organizations have raised over $4.5 million dollars from
their sponsorship of the subsequent thirty-one
Decorators' ShowHouses. In 1994, when the
Symphony Volunteer Council pledged two mil-
lion dollars to the Alabama Symphonic Association's Endowment Fund, subsequent Decorators' ShowHouses have raised nearly 100%
of that pledge. Email: info@SymphonyVolun-
teerCouncil.org
Birmingham, Alabama, Donnachaidh-Roberts
Estate of Jemison Park

The Designer Showhouse of New Jersey –
www.humcfoundation.com
This annual event benefits the John Theurer
Cancer Center at Hackensack University
Medical Center. The event enlists the talents
of some of the top interior and landscape

designers from the Garden State and New York City. For more information call 201-996-3252. Email: www.humcfoundation.com/site/PageNavigator/designer_showhouse08
20 Dennison Drive East, Saddle River, New Jersey

Hampton Designer Showhouse, Sagaponic, New York – info@hamptondesignershowhouse.com
This annual event creates a dream home, enlisting designers to celebrities to create signature looks. Proceeds benefit the Southampton Hospital. For more information, visit www.hamptondesignershowhouse.com. Mitchell Manning Associates, 212-980-1700

Jacksonville Symphony Guild-Designer Show House & Garden – www.collierclassichomes.com
Pablo Creek Reserve, Jacksonville, Florida. Built by Collier Classic Homes and was a detailed English Country Manor (6,252 SF).

Junior League of Greater Princeton Showhouse – www.jlgp.org
This annual event raises funds for this area chapter of the international Junior League organizations that foster a spirit of volunteerism in women over the age of twenty-one. The league is dedicated to improving communities through effective action and leadership. The Princeton league works to increase literacy skills in young children and their parents. 2008 Drake's Corner Showhouse

Junior League of Montclair Showhouse – www.jlgp.org
The Junior League of Montclair is a nonprofit organization of trained volunteers. Through hands-on projects and partnerships, our 500 members build a better community by promoting education, health and wellness, literacy and the arts for over 5,000 children at risk each year.

Kips Bay Decorator Showhouse – www.kipsbay.org
For almost four decades, this annual, premier decorator event has been launched to benefit the Kips Bay Boys and Girls Club located in the Southeast Bronx, New York. For over ninety-two years, Kips Bay has played a critical role in helping to shape the lives of thousands of young children throughout the New York metropolitan area.

Lane Estate Showhouse – www.2008designer showhouse.com
The Lane Estate Showhouse was launched by Syd and Deb Dufton. It is not an annual event yet, but they are scouting locations for an event in 2010. The event benefited, in part, local breast cancer charities. Phone: 631-734-5894, email: info@2008designershowhouse.com

Malcolm House Designer Showcase – www.nassaucountyny.gov/agencies/Parks/Wheretogo/museums/index.html
In 2005, the non-profit Nassau Conservancy in New York organized a showhouse in the Historic Malcolm House on Jericho Preserve, working with 16 Long Island Designers to refurbish and renovate the property and open it for a special designer showcase. (Harrison Hunt, Nassau Conservancy at 571-7631 or Malcolm House directly at 571-7064.)

Mansion in May – www.wammh.com
This event takes place every other year and is sponsored by the Women's Association of Morristown Memorial Hospital to raise funds for specific hospital projects. The month long event with 18,000 visitors is run completely by over 1000 volunteers. (Contact: Katherine Sheeleigh, email: mansioninmaypr@gmail.com)

Mansions & Millionaires Designers Showcase™
This twice annual, spring and fall event showcases designers and artisans work and benefits various charities and organizations. The seasonal events are focused mainly on mansions along Long Island's "Gold Coast" or north shore, where many once-prosperous properties await a face-lift. The event offers restoration along with beautification. Recent events have been held at and benefited properties owned by the The Caumsett Foundation, Caumsett State Historic Park, Lloyd Neck, New York, Nassau County's The Hempstead House, The Lindens, Lloyd Harbor Showhouse, Chelsea Manor, Chelsea Seats Showhouse, Sandy Point Preserve, Bailey Manor, Contacts: Arlene Travis and Carol Aaronsen, 516-671-1313 (mansionlady@gmail.com, fax: 516-671-1376).

Merrywood Designer Showhouse – www.
homeresourceguide.com/merrywood.html
The Merrywood Designer Show House was held in Greenwich, Connecticut, in 2006, to benefit the Greenwich Family Y's capital campaign for the expansion and upgrading of the YMCA building, a cherished Greenwich Landmark. Over thirty regional designers decorated a 20,000 square foot mansion in grand fashion for this public showcase.

National Symphony Orchestra Celebrations – www.kennedy-center.org/nso/support/auxiliary/celebration
The Women's Committee for the National Symphony Orchestra was pleased to announce its second annual Celebrations fundraiser: Beyond Dragons: An East-West Fusion of Interior Design. The five day Asian-inspired interior design show featured innovative room designs created by some of Washington's top noted designers. From the subtle to the dramatic, Beyond Dragons offered inspiration to those who are seeking to create spaces in their homes which reflect the Asian concepts of balance and harmony, color and texture, simplicity and richness while maintaining the comfort and familiarity of western classic and modern traditions. The event also featured seminars on entertaining and decorating, feng shui, special cultural presentations and hosts some of the area's most coveted shopping boutiques. This is an event sponsored by The Women's Committee for the National Symphony Orchestra; proceeds from the event are used to buy small instruments for educational programs that help familiarize children with the national symphony.

Orchard Hill Designer Showhouse – www.oldwestburygardens.org
Held in June 2008, this event benefited its host, Old Westbury Gardens in New York, a National Register of Historic Places estate that functions as a museum and public garden. For more information, contact Mitchell Manning Associates, 212-980-1711, www.orchardhilldesignershowhouse.com

Saratoga Builders Association Showcase of Homes – www.saratogabuilders.org
This annual event draws thousands of people to tour a number of houses each year. The event is organized by the builder's association, a trade association that represents builders, developers, suppliers, subcontractors, architects, engineers, realtors, attorneys, financers, and other industry professionals. Proceeds benefit Habitat for Humanity and Rebuilding Together.

Scarsdale Show House – www.scarsdalewomansclub.org
The Scarsdale Woman's Club has managed the historic Rowley Estate since 1928. In 2005 they teamed up with the New York metropolitan chapter of the American Society of Interior Designers to host an event that resulted in a dramatic makeover for the manor house, and offered visitors a chance to tour the property. Proceeds benefited the American Cancer Society and several philanthropic projects sponsored by the club.

St. Matthews Episcopal Day School Dickens House – www.stmatthewsday.org/develop/Dickens-House

Dickens House has been the major fundraising event for St. Matthew's Episcopal Day School in Hillsborough, California, for over twenty years. The show house and holiday boutique has a major presence and following on the Peninsula and beyond. This event is made possible through the collaborative volunteer efforts of the many dedicated St. Matthew's parents and students, extended families and friends of the school. All of the proceeds from Dickens House assist the Day School in furthering its mission to offer an enriched academic and social program to students from the surrounding Peninsula communities. All funds raised through sponsorship of the Opening Night Premiere Party are used to support student financial assistance.

Stately Homes by the Sea Designer Showhouse – www.statelyhomesbythesea.com

Founded in 1912, Visiting Nurse Association of Central Jersey (VNACJ) is the largest voluntary, nonprofit home care agency in New Jersey, serving more than 100,000 individuals each year in Monmouth, Middlesex, and Ocean counties.

The proceeds from Stately Homes By-The-Sea Show House Events are used to benefit VNACJ home care, hospice, and community-based programs and services. In 2007 over $1.1 million in charitable care was provided to individuals and underinsured community-based programs. Phone: 800-862-3330

Tucson Museum of Art Designer Showhouse – www.TucsonMuseumofArt.org

Sponsored by the Tucson Museum of Art League and Tucson Home Magazine, this event raised money for the museum and its many community and educational programs.

Twin Maples Centennial Showhouse – www.historictwinmaples.org

This lavish public event was held in 2008 to restore the historic Twin Maples estate in Summit, New Jersey. The beautiful home, listed on the National Register of Historic Places, has been headquarters for The Fortnightly Club and The Summit Junior Fortnightly Club since 1949. These two groups organize and host numerous charitable functions for good causes. Email: amandaford@historictwinmaples.org

Vanguard Designer Showhouse – www.vanguardshowhouse.org

This annual event benefits the Albany Symphony Orchestra in Albany, New York. Vanguard is an all-volunteer organization, which exists to support the Albany Symphony Orchestra. Its chief fund-raiser is its annual Designer Showhouse, which is almost three decades old. Email: www.albanysymphony.com. Ruth Cook, President. Phone: 518-664-5122.

Photographers

Alanna Smith Photographer
Soul Shine Galleries
www.soulshinegalleries.com

Charles Meacham
Malvern, Pennsylvania
610-935-9196

Chelsea Photographic
Bob Pearce ABIPP
904-399-3939

Dan Muro
Fast Forward Unlimited
www.fastforwardunlimited.com

David R. Sloane Photography
New Canaan, Connecticut
203-966-0408

Derek Wiesahahn
New York Spaces
www.nyspacesmagazine.com

Dustin Peck Photography, Inc.
Charlotte, North Carolina
www.dustinpeckphotography.com

Emily Gilbert Photography
www.emilygilbertphotography.com
917-816-0690

Geanine Palmer
Miller Place, NY
631-209-1500

Greg Lanza
New York, New York
www.greglanzadesign.com

Ivy D Photography, Inc.
Levittown, New York
www.ivydphotography.com

Jack Ader
Images for Presentation
imagesforpres@aol.com

Jeff White Photography
www.jeffwhitephotographer.com
256-651-8079

John Armich Photography
Alburtis, Pennsylvania
www.johnarmich.com

John J. Coyle Jr.
Coyle Commercial Photographic Studios
410.825.6858

Ken Hild Photography
Port Jefferson, New York
631-846-6896

Kris Tamburello
www.Kristamburello.com

Marisa Pellegrini
www.marisapellegrini.com
646-296-7762

Peter Kutcher Photography
Long Island, New York

Phillip Ennis
www.phillip-ennis.com
914-234-9574

Peter Paige
201-236-8730
www.peterpaige.com

Peter Rymwid
973-628-1527
www.peterrymwid.com

Pieter Estersohn Photography
www.pieterestersohn.com

Decorative Painters

Randall Perry
Schaghticoke, New York
www.randallperry.com

Reflex Photo
Steve Geraci
631-567-8777

Scott Moore
www.scottmoorephoto.com
902-371-6439

Susan Munroe
www.susanmunroephoto.com

Tim Ebert
Northport, New York
516-587-2583

Tim Fuller
www.timfuller.com
520-622-3900

Tom Grimes
www.tomgrimes.com
917-570-1823

Viewpiont Photography
Pam Setchell
www.viewpointphotography.com

Vinnie Fish
VirginiaFish@att.net

Wing Wong, Memories TTL, LLC
Rutherford, New Jersey
www.memoriesttl.com

William Busch
Busch Studios
Oyster Bay, New York

Michael Goldberg
Classic Décor
Fair Lawn, New Jersey
www.theclassicdecor.com

Mary Korzinski
Custom Design Associates
Clifton Park, New York
www.customdesignassociates.com

Lou Lou's Whimsicals
Unionville, Pennsylvania
www.loulouswhimsicals.com

Sal and Nancy Moccia
Locust Valley, New York
516-609-3363

Monique
East Northport, New York
www.inspiredillusionsbymonique.com

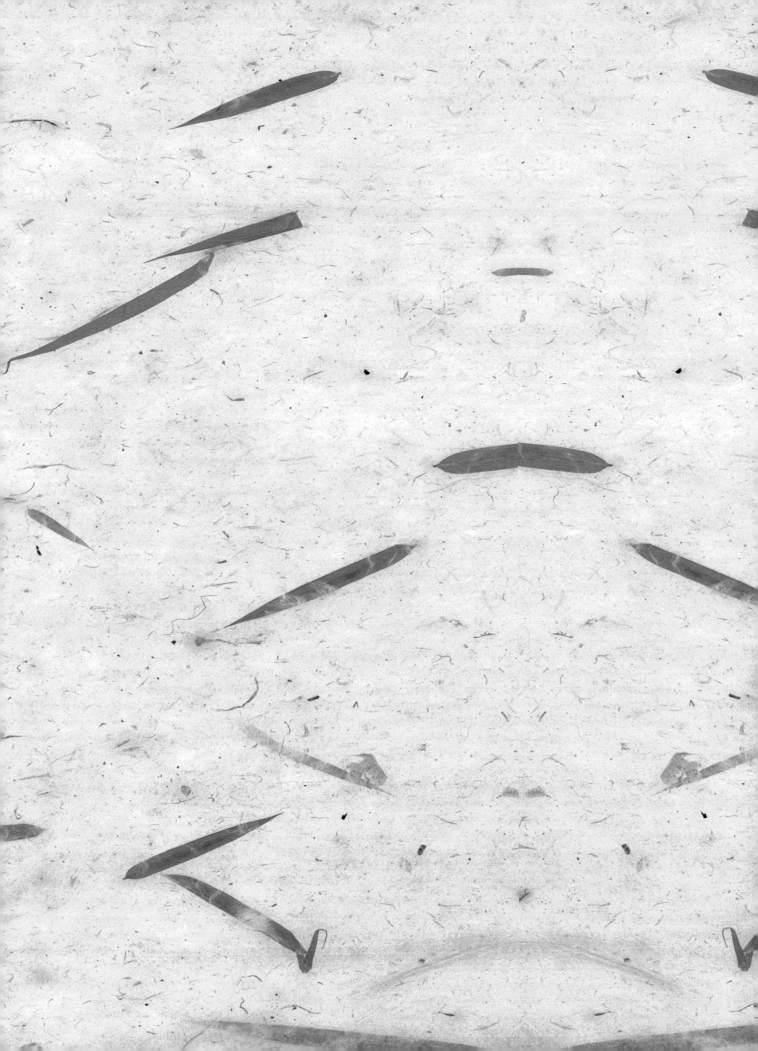